Bahá'í Coloring Book for Families & Children

Compiled and Illustrated By Jesica Marie Nkouaga

Acknowledgements

Thank you to Katie Thoennes for her help with formatting the cover and back cover. Thank you to Once Voice Press for the original printing of this title, and for giving me the confidence to continue creating books for children. Thank you to Bahá'í Writings for the spiritually uplifting quotations.

Bahá'í Coloring Book for Families & Children
Jesica Marie Nkouaga

Illustrations copyright © 2019 by Jesica Nkouaga

All rights reserved. Except as permitted under U.S. Copyright Act of 1976, no part of this publication may be reproduce, distributed, or transmitted in any form or by any means, or stored in a database or retrieval system, without the prior written permission of the author. For information regarding permission, contact Jesica Nkouaga at emmanuelandthehedgehog@gmail.com

Permission is granted to teachers to make limited copies of individual pages for classroom use.

Bahá'í Writings copyright © Bahá'í International Community, various dates.

ISBN-13: 978-0-578-59055-4

Originally Published by One Voice Press, LLC
Essex, Maryland, USA
First Printed: September 2012
10 9 8 7 6 5 4 3 2

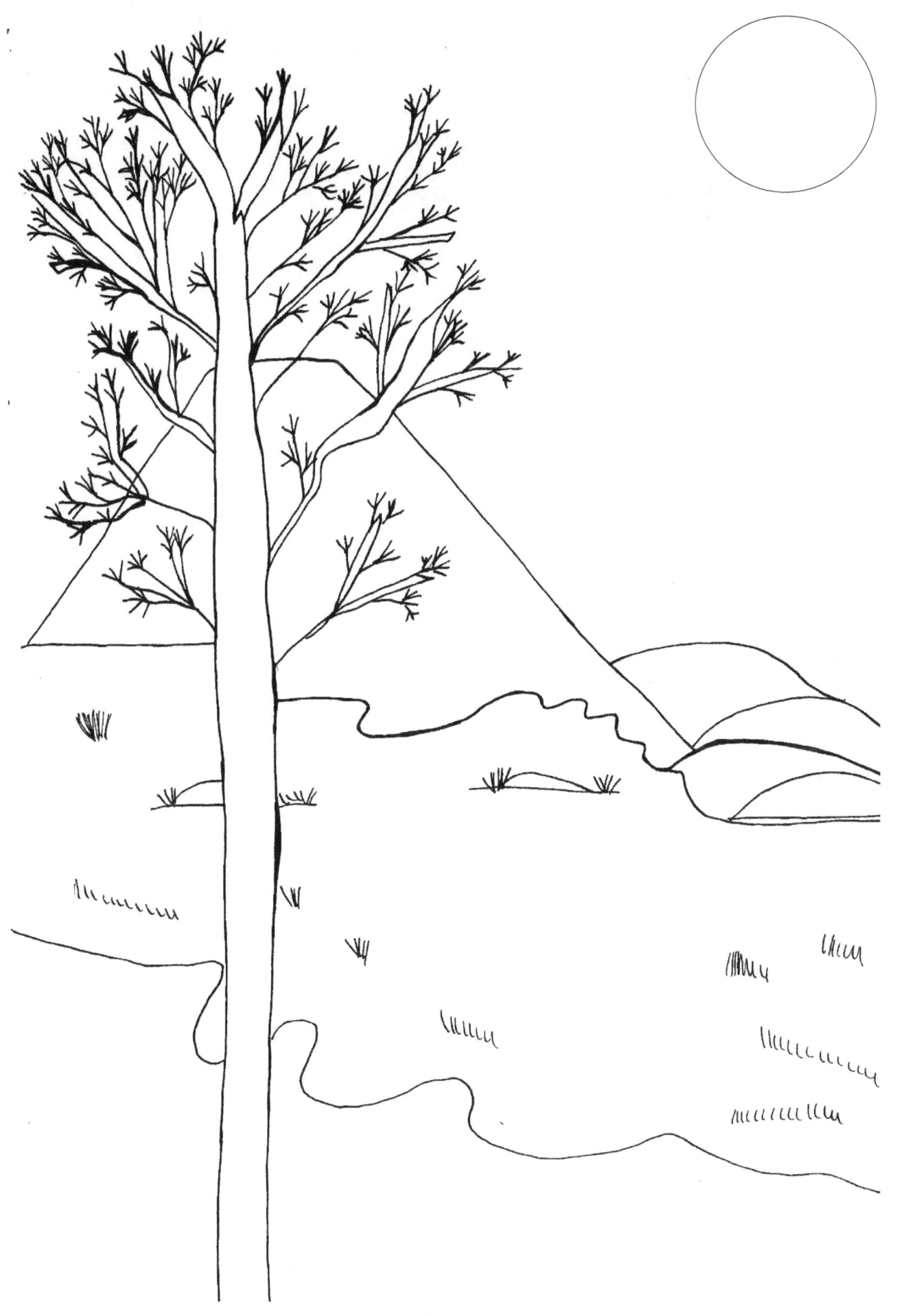

The earth is but one country and mankind its citizens. [1]

Music is an important means to the education and development of humanity... [2]

It is the hope of 'Abdu'l-Baha that those youthful souls . . .
will be tended by one who traineth them to love. ³

Regard man as a mine rich in gems of inestimable value. Education can, alone, cause it to reveal its treasures, and enable mankind to benefit. [4]

O well-beloved ones! The tabernacle of unity hath been raised; regard ye not one another as strangers. Ye are the fruits of one tree, and the leaves of one branch. 5

The source of crafts, sciences and arts is the power of reflection. 6

When a man turns his face to God he finds sunshine everywhere. 7

I charge you all that each one of you concentrate all the thoughts of your heart on love and unity . . . Thoughts of love are constructive of brotherhood, peace, friendship, and happiness. 8

O God! Protect these children, graciously assist them to be educated and enable them to render service to the world of humanity. 9

May you pursue your education and training for future service to mankind. 10

Work done in the spirit of service is the highest form of worship. [11]

While the children are yet in their infancy feed them from the breast of heavenly grace, foster them in the cradle of all excellence. 12

A child is as a young plant: it will grow in whatever way you train it. If you rear it to be truthful, and kind, and righteous, it will grow straight, it will be fresh and tender, and will flourish...[13]

If an animal is sick they should endeavor to cure it; if it is hungry, they should feed it, if it is thirsty, they should satisfy its thirst, if it is tired, they should give it rest.

To the blessed animal . . . The utmost kindness should be exercised; the more the better it will be. 15

If love and agreement are manifest in a single family, that family will advance, become illumined and spiritual. 16

Be obedient and kind to thy father and mother. 17

You must have infinite love for each other, each preferring the other before himself. 18

Joy gives us wings! In times of joy our strength is more vital, our intellect keener, and our understanding less clouded. 19

It is incumbent upon everyone to show the utmost love
. . . And sincere kindliness unto all the people and
kindreds of the world, be they friends or strangers. [20]

Let them strive by day and by night to establish within their children faith and certitude, the fear of God, the love of the Beloved of the worlds, and all good qualities and traits. 21

...Mothers are the first educators, the first mentors; and truly it is the mothers who determine the happiness, the future greatness, the courteous ways and learning and judgment, the understanding and the faith of their little ones. 22

Let the mothers consider that whatever concerneth the education of children is of the first importance. Let them put forth every effort in this regard, for when the bough is green and tender it will grow in whatever way ye train it...[23]

It is clear...that the future generation depends on the mothers of today. 24

Bibliography

1. Bahá'u'lláh, *Gleanings from the Writings of Bahá'u'lláh*, p. 250.
2. 'Abdu'l-Bahá, *Lights of Guidance*, 410.
3. 'Abdu'l-Bahá, *Selections from the Writings of 'Abdu'l-Bahá*, p. 134.
4. Bahá'u'lláh, *Gleanings from the Writings of Bahá'u'lláh*, p. 259.
5. Bahá'u'lláh, *Tablets of Bahá'u'lláh,* p. 164.
6. Bahá'u'lláh, *Tablets of Bahá'u'lláh,* p. 72.
7. 'Abdu'l-Bahá, *Bahá'í Revelation,* pp. 301-2.
8. 'Abdu'l-Bahá, *Paris Talks*, p. 29.
9. 'Abdu'l-Bahá, *Bahá'í Prayers, p. 35.*
10. Universal House of Justice, *Lights of Guidance,* p. 635.
11. 'Abdu'l-Bahá, *Bahá'í Education: A Compilation,* p. 77.
12. 'Abdu'l-Bahá, *Selections from the Writings of 'Abdu'l-Bahá*, p. 129.
13. 'Abdu'l-Bahá, *Compilation*, vol. I, p. 287.
14. 'Abdu'l-Bahá, *Bahá'í Revelation,* p. 303.
15. 'Abdu'l-Bahá, *Bahá'í Revelation,* p. 303.
16. 'Abdu'l-Bahá, *Bahá'í World Faith,* p. 229.
17. 'Abdu'l-Bahá, *Bahá'í World,* vol. XII, p. 896.
18. 'Abdu'l-Bahá, *The Promulgation of Universal Peace,* p. 218.
19. 'Abdu'l-Bahá, *Paris Talks*, p. 109.
20. 'Abdu'l-Bahá, *Will and Testament of 'Abdu'l-Bahá,* p. 13.
21. 'Abdu'l-Bahá, *Selections from the Writings of 'Abdu'l-Bahá*, p. 125.
22. 'Abdu'l-Bahá, *Selections from the Writings of 'Abdu'l-Bahá*, p. 126.
23. 'Abdu'l-Bahá, *Selections from the Writings of 'Abdu'l-Bahá*, p. 125.
24. 'Abdu'l-Bahá, *Paris Talks*, p. 162.

About the Illustrator

Jesica Nkouaga grew up on a dairy farm in rural Minnesota. She has earned a Bachelor of Arts in Global Studies and a Master of Liberal Studies in ESOL education. As an educator, she has volunteered and taught in six different countries. Jesica gains inspiration from the Bahá'í Faith and its message of unity as well as children and nature.

www.ingramcontent.com/pod-product-compliance
Lightning Source LLC
Chambersburg PA
CBHW081157290426

44108CB00018B/2586